Curriculum

they put
on masks

they put
on masks

BYRD BAYLOR

illustrated by
JERRY INGRAM

CHARLES SCRIBNER'S SONS • NEW YORK

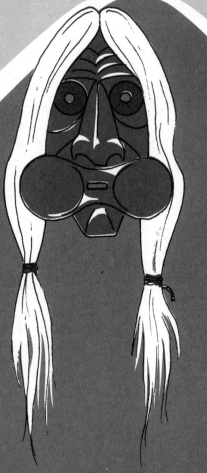

Text copyright © 1974 Byrd Baylor
Illustrations copyright © 1974 Jerry Ingram

This book published simultaneously in the
United States of America and in Canada—
Copyright under the Berne Convention

5 7 9 11 13 15 17 19 RD/C 20 18 16 14 12 10 8 6 4

Printed in the United States of America
Library of Congress Catalog Card Number 73-19557
SBN 684-13767-4

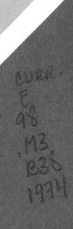

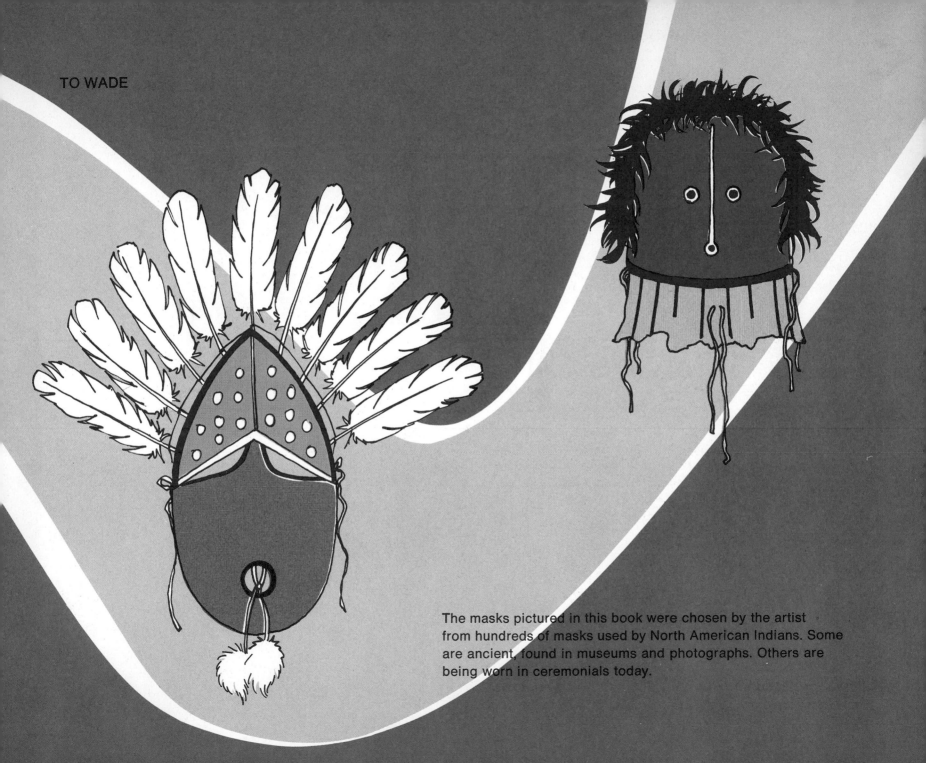

TO WADE

The masks pictured in this book were chosen by the artist from hundreds of masks used by North American Indians. Some are ancient, found in museums and photographs. Others are being worn in ceremonials today.

They made their masks of
wood
and deerskin
and seashells
and cornhusks
and horsehair
and bones.

Yes,
and they made them of
magic
and dreams
and the oldest dark secrets
of life.

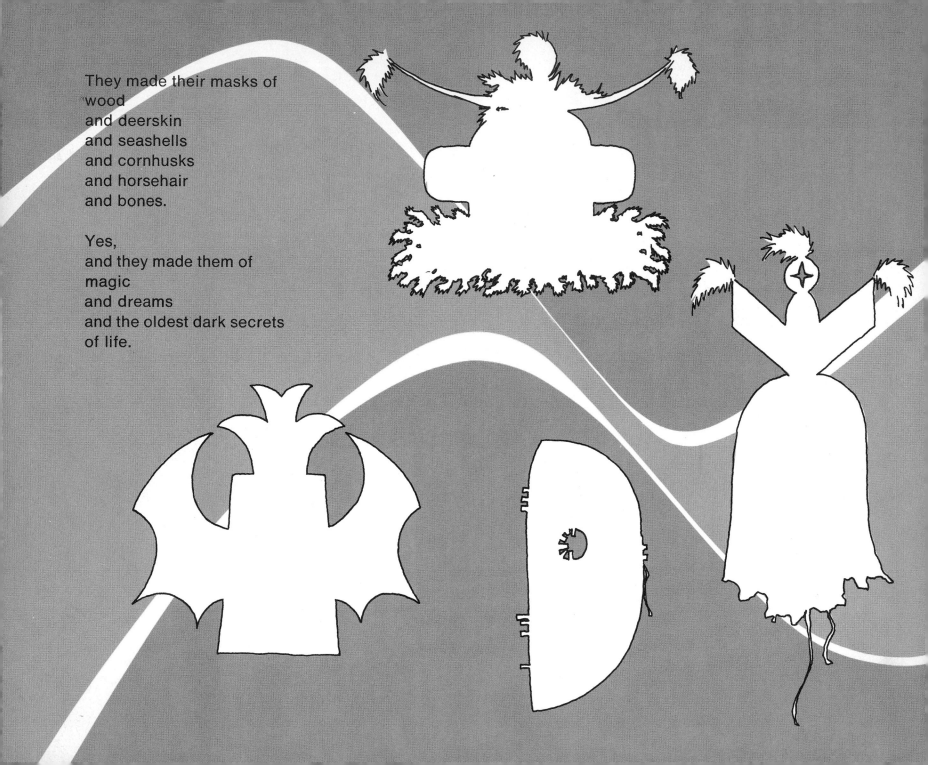

They made masks of
beads
and string
and ivory
and turquoise
and flowers.

Yes,
and they made them of
wishes
and hunger
and thirst
and they even made them
of prayers.

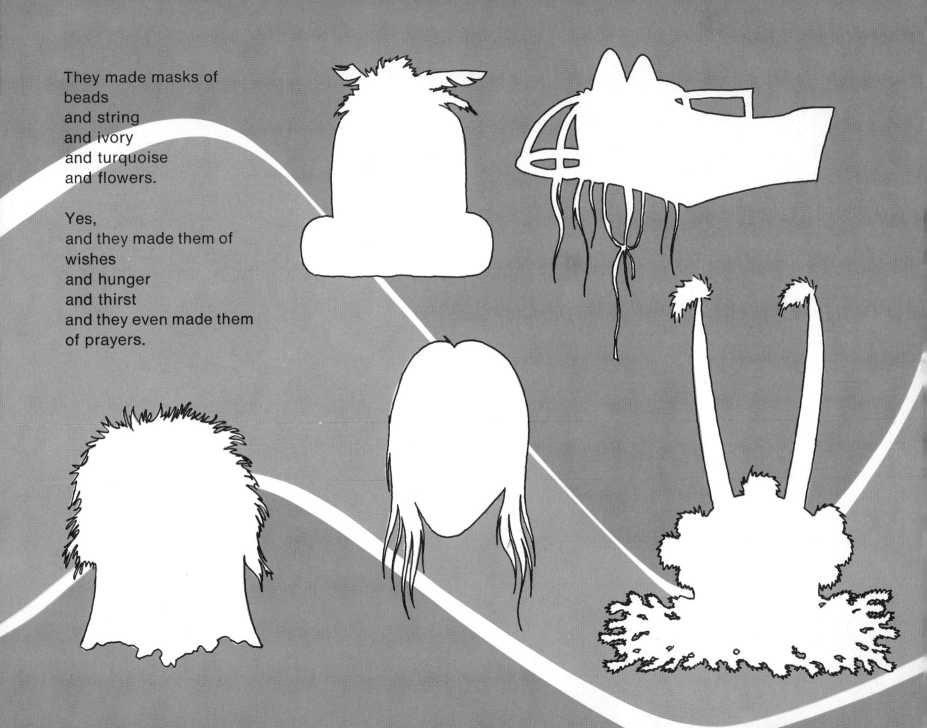

Think of those first Indian tribes
wandering in a hard, wild, lonely land.

They must have wondered how
to make rain fall
and seeds grow
and how to find the animals
they hunted in the hills
and how to overcome their enemies
and how to make sick children well again.

They needed ways to bring good luck.
Without good luck
how could they even live from day to day?

So each tribe spoke to the great fierce gods
of lightning and thunder and rain and sun.

How?
They put on masks
and they made dances
and music and songs.

They wanted their ceremonies
to be so powerful
and so beautiful
that all the gods
would *have* to listen
and be pleased.

8

The Indians said
a mask can change you
into the Spirit of Thunder—
into ANYTHING.
You can be Mother of the Earth,
the Maker of Stars,
the Killer of Monsters—
ANYTHING.
You can be the Spirit of
All Growing Things.
You can be
ANYTHING AT ALL.

Even now
there are Indian tribes
that have not forgotten
what their grandfathers
and great-grandfathers
knew.

They still feel
the power
in their masks.
They use them
in the ancient
sacred ways.

In his far white icy world
the Eskimo honors the spirits of
all the animals and fish and birds
that he must hunt to live.

He sings magically for
walrus and seal and caribou.
He tries to please the angry spirits
of the sea.
He asks them to watch over
the helpless men
in their small boats.

He sings for the Old Woman
Who Lives in the Sea
and he sings for the Spirit of
Cold Weather and Storms.
He makes masks for
the Bad Spirit of the Mountain
and for the Good Spirit of Driftwood.
He doesn't forget Sun Sister.

His masks all come from dreams.
They have to be carved
just the way they were dreamed.
And Eskimo masks always keep
the look of dreams
about them . . .

dreams made of driftwood,
dreams decorated with porcupine quills
and reindeer hair and willow bark.
Sometimes there's ivory,
sometimes beads,
maybe circles of thin curved whalebone
and feathers.
You use whatever was there
in the dream.

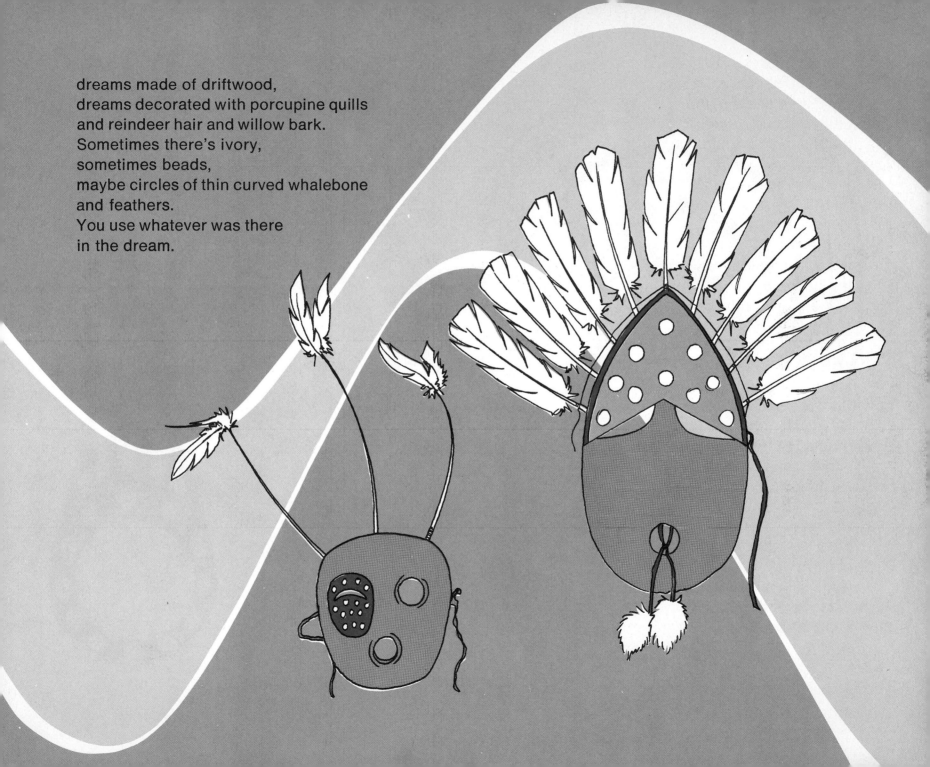

These masks are
so magical
the carver himself
has to touch them
carefully.

He tries to finish his work
on the day he begins it.
Then he hides that mask away
in a dark secret spot of his own
and when he carries it
to the ceremonial place
he hides it under his clothing
and he goes at night.

At last a dancer puts on the mask.
When he begins to move.
he moves in a new way.
He moves the way
a spirit moves.

He has forgotten
he's a man.
He cries out in a spirit voice—
Eeeeeeeee..... Eeeeeeeee.....

Listen,
someone is singing:

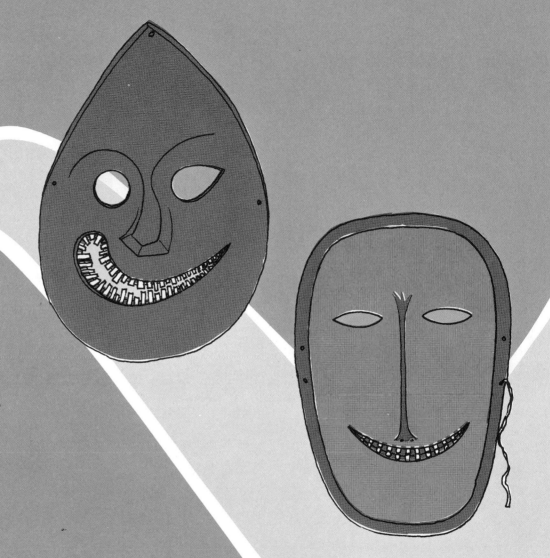

Let me move my face, let me dance,
Let me shrug my shoulders, let me shake my body.
Let me fold my arms, let me crouch down.
Let me hold my hands under my chin.

South of the Eskimos,
along the Northwest Coast,
other great ceremonies
must have shaken the
rainy cedar forests,
must have been heard by
beaver and bear and eagle,
must have rung out over
the rocky coast of the Pacific
and reached whale and salmon
there in the saltwater ocean.

When you see the masks
these people used
you know why the carvers
had to be artists.
You know why they were paid
in furs and shells and long canoes
and feasts that lasted for days.
The carver of masks was a famous man.

No wonder.
Look at those masks.

The eyes glisten with abalone shell.
Cedar bark hangs down in long swinging strips.
There is fur and hammered copper.
And bird beaks rattle when the mask moves.

These masks honor the clan ancestors
of the people,
the long ago heroes of their stories
and the spirit birds and spirit animals
they came from.

If you belong to the clan of
the KILLER WHALE
then all the songs and dances
and masks of KILLER WHALE
are *your* songs and dances and masks.
You ask special favors
of your great ancestor,
KILLER WHALE.

Or if WOLF is your ancestor
you ask his help
in times of trouble.
You honor him with a great
WOLF mask.

The Kwakiutl Indians
remember these things.
Even now
they sometimes make a mask
so large
only the strongest dancer
can wear it.
Imagine a bird that fills the sky.
The beak alone is as large as a man.

Is it magic?
Or does the dancer under the mask
pull hidden strings
to make that huge beak swing open
and close again with a clacking sound?

Who wouldn't move back into the shadows
when that clack-clack-clack comes near?

Now
they're singing to one
who has the power to turn back storms:

You, whose day it is,
Make it beautiful.
Get out your rainbow colors
So it will be beautiful.

17

On the other side of the country,
among the grassy hills and woodlands
of the Northeast,
the Iroquois still speak
of False Face.

There never was sickness
in the world,
they say,
until that evil spirit
brought it.

They tell their children
of the days
at the beginning of the world
when the tribe's first hero
battled against False Face.
They say he fought so fiercely
a mountain fell on that bad spirit.

No wonder False Face masks
look twisted
and crooked
and shaken
and wildly surprised.
How else would you look
if a mountain had fallen
on *you*?

18

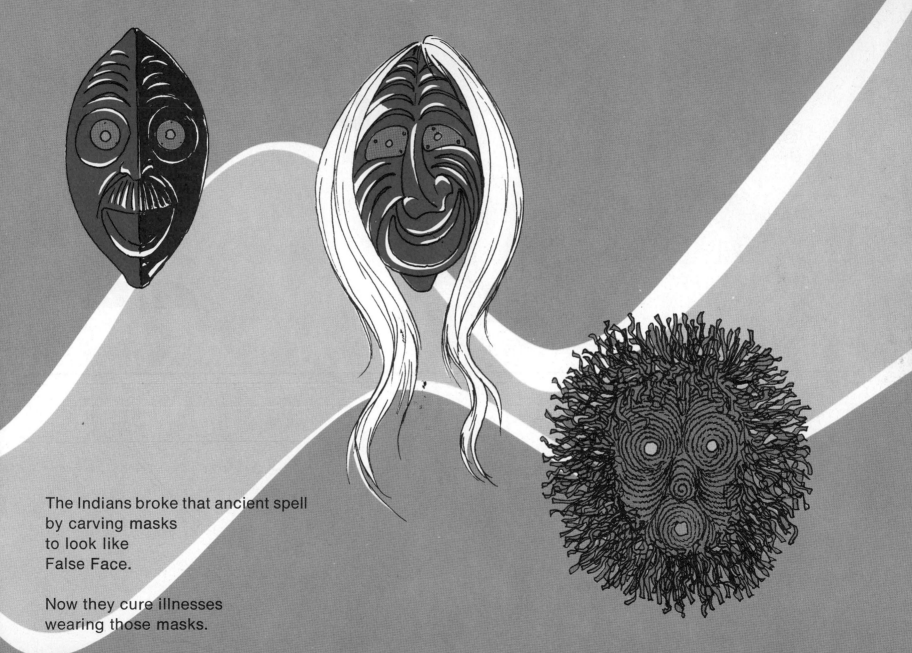

The Indians broke that ancient spell
by carving masks
to look like
False Face.

Now they cure illnesses
wearing those masks.

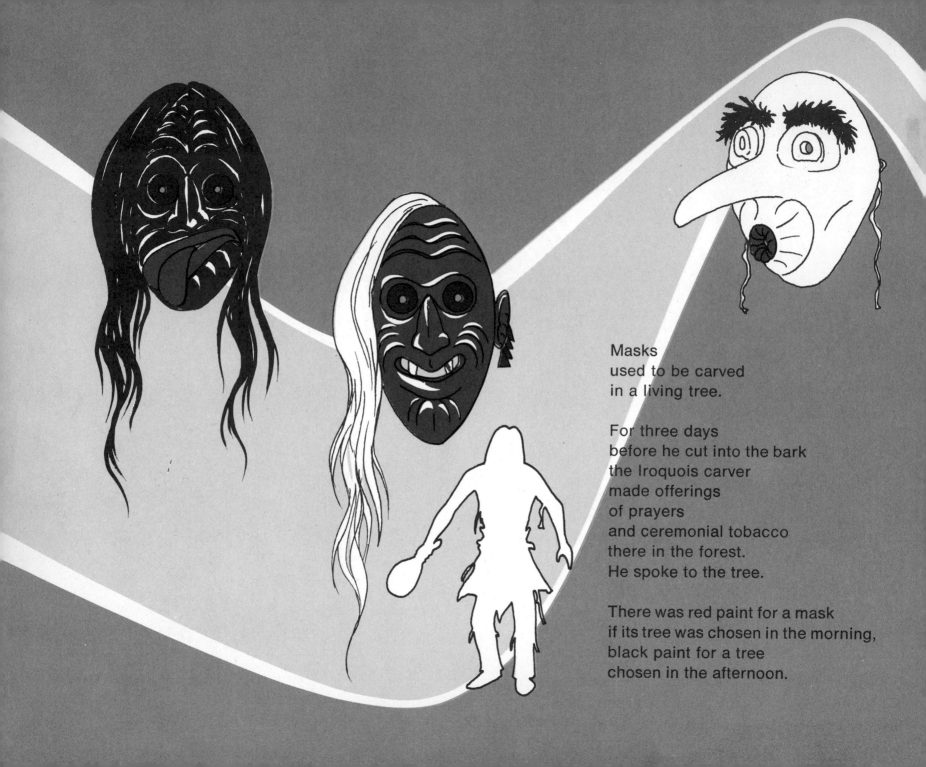

Masks
used to be carved
in a living tree.

For three days
before he cut into the bark
the Iroquois carver
made offerings
of prayers
and ceremonial tobacco
there in the forest.
He spoke to the tree.

There was red paint for a mask
if its tree was chosen in the morning,
black paint for a tree
chosen in the afternoon.

Pieces of metal
around the eyes
glisten and shine as
the dancer leaps and sways
in the dim firelight.

The Iroquois had something else
to make masks with—
corn.
They braided the dry pale husks
and sewed the braids
in a circle-face.

Corn—
for nothing is more sacred
than corn.

They sang to the Four Winds
and to the Thunders.
They said the Thunder gods
were birds with flashing eyes.

Sometimes they chanted
in these words:

Help in our night journey
Now no sun is shining.
Now no star is glowing.
Come show us the pathway.

In the dry bright open land
of the Southwest
Indians have always been
brother and sister to
rocks and plants
and rain and sand
and fox and deer
and lizard and spider and bird.

The earth belongs
to every living thing,
not just to man, they say.

That's why their masks
and dances and songs
draw all these parts of life
together—
even the life in stones,
the life in wind.

Navajo Indians know
that if you are unhappy
or if you have bad thoughts
or bad dreams
or if you are out of luck
and everything you try goes wrong
or if you have an illness—
then you are not in harmony
with the other parts of the world.

22

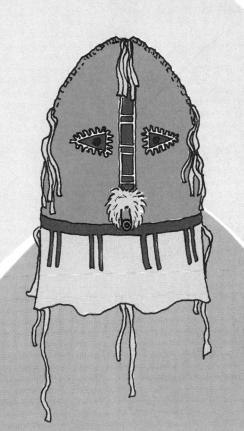

Maybe you need
the Blessing Way Ceremony,
maybe the Mountain Way
or the Shooting Star Chant,
maybe the Night Chant
to fill you with good again,
to turn you toward the Beauty Path.

Chants and music and sand paintings and sacred pollen
and masked dancers all bring their mysterious blessings.

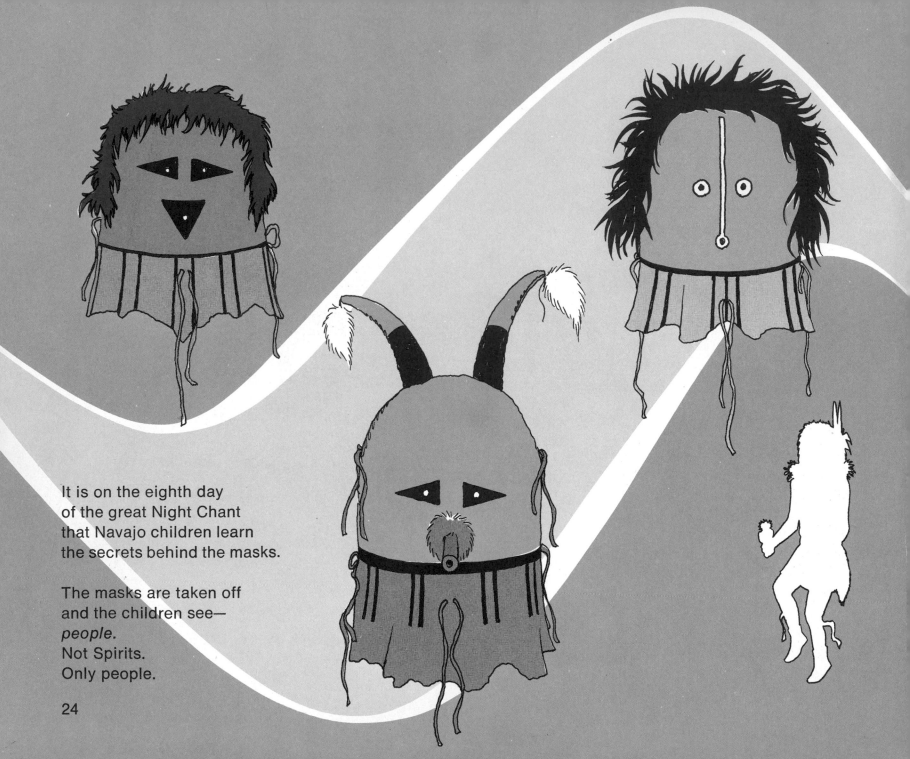

It is on the eighth day
of the great Night Chant
that Navajo children learn
the secrets behind the masks.

The masks are taken off
and the children see—
people.
Not Spirits.
Only people.

24

The masks are put on the children then
so each one sees the world through the eyes of
the Yeibichais.

Talking God of the East puts his mask
on a small dark boy.

The child who
touches that mask to his face
feels its power cover him . . .

just as everyone who watches
feels the power
and the blessings
cover
the people.

Now the one who needed help
can say again:

In Beauty I walk.
With Beauty before me I walk.
With Beauty behind me I walk.
With Beauty above me I walk.
It is finished in Beauty. . . .

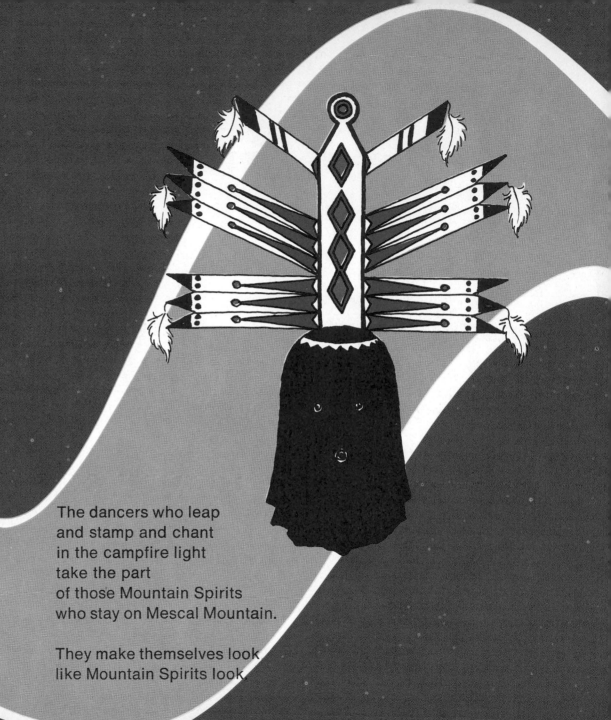

The Apaches look
off in the distance
and see the mountains rising
strong and shadowy
above them.

They know that there
where the spruce grows thick
the Mountain Spirits live
among the cliffs and caves
of the mountaintop.

These Mountain Spirits
do not forget their people.
They send rain
and happiness
and long life
to the Apaches.

And the Apaches do not forget
the Mountain Spirits.

When a girl changes
from child to woman
her people
have a ceremony
to bring her blessings,
to wish her well
on her long life journey.

The dancers who leap
and stamp and chant
in the campfire light
take the part
of those Mountain Spirits
who stay on Mescal Mountain.

They make themselves look
like Mountain Spirits look.

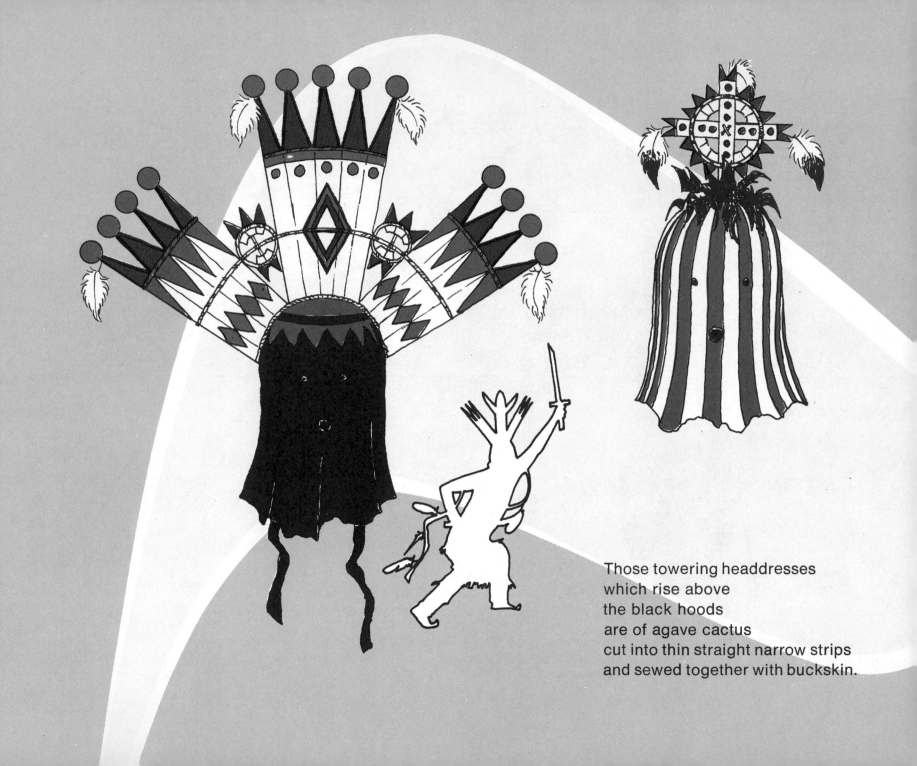

Those towering headdresses
which rise above
the black hoods
are of agave cactus
cut into thin straight narrow strips
and sewed together with buckskin.

The colors
are the bright clear colors of
the four sacred directions—
white for north
black for east
blue for south
yellow for west.
They are the colors of
sky and sun
and earth and seeds
and clouds and thunder,
the colors of happiness,
the colors of life.

High on Mescal Mountain
the Mountain Spirits
look down over their people
and watch the dancers
and hear this song:

All the bad things
that used to be
vanished.
All the bad wishes
that were in the world
vanished.
The lightning struck four times for them.
It struck four times for me.

From the high rocky Hopi mesas
down to the Rio Grande Valley
children in quiet dry earth-colored
Pueblo villages
grow up seeing
kachinas dance
in the same village plazas
where their ancestors
saw kachinas dance.

There are
Buffalo Dances . . .
for the buffalo is a sacred animal.

Eagle Dances . . .
for the eagle flies out of sight
toward the sun.
Even its feathers
are blessings.

Parrot Dances . . .
for the parrot comes
from far away
and looks into the sun
without blinking.

Corn Dances . . .
for corn is
the sacred Corn Mother.

Every Pueblo tribe
has its own dances
but every dance
in every village
is a dance about
being alive.
Each one says
live
and *grow*
and *feel*
and *be*.

30

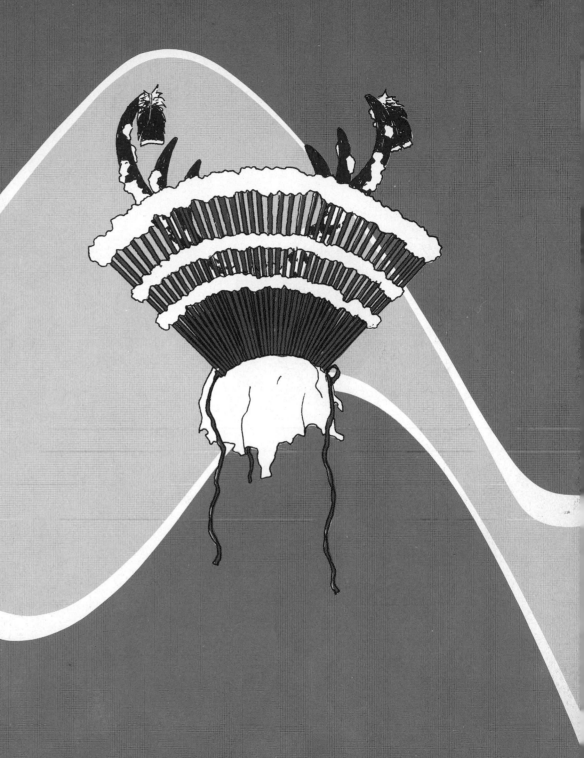

In every village
the sounds and the movements
of the dancers
are borrowed from
the things of the earth—
from clouds and winds
and from rain falling
and from the leaping of deer
and the howling of wolves
and the flight of birds in an open sky
and from seeds sprouting
and from leaves unfolding—
from everything life touches.

And every song,
every beat of the drums,
every shake of the rattles,
every design on a mask
is a call for rain
because here
in the dry Southwest
rain is
life.

Hopi children
like that time
in summer
when the first corn is ripe
and the kachinas
are ready to go back
to their home
in the San Francisco Peaks.

But before they go
there is one more ceremony.
They call it Niman,
the Home Dance.

Long lines of
slow, powerful kachinas
dance all day in the
sunlight of the plaza.

Their colors are the brightest colors
in the world.
Their masks
are topped with feathers
and tall grass
and painted butterflies
and rainbows
and corn and clouds
and there is green spruce
around their necks
and their bodies glow.

The people have gifts and blessings
for the kachinas
and the kachinas
have gifts and blessings
for the people.

35

Kachinas give
corn and melons
and Hopi bread
and baskets.

Special presents for children—
rattles and kachina dolls
carved from the roots of cottonwood trees,
bows and arrows
and bulrushes which are tender and sweet
to be chewed like gum.

No child
forgets
the moment
when a kachina
reaches down
to put a gift
into his hands.

Sometimes he hears words
that aren't from any language.
Sometimes they are words
that seem to come up
from the earth:

kyal ee see ee
a angwee ee ee
ò òn nà nèe ee ee
klù ee toè o ùh.

37

In another Pueblo village
the Zuni Indians wait
for the coldest days of winter.
That's the time
six huge birdlike kachinas
come to move among
the people
and bless their houses
and bless their lives.

They call them
Shalakos . . .
those giants
ten feet tall.
They go swaying
and dipping,
gliding,
half flying,
half floating.

Can you hear the strange
whistling sounds they make?

Look at their buffalo horns,
the bird beaks that snap and clack,
the turquoise blue masks,
the bulging eyes,
the long black hair,
the raven feathers
that circle their throats.

38

Shalakos are
the messengers
of the gods.
Before they go back
to their home in Blue Lake
they race across a field
to show the people
how swiftly
their prayers for rain
are carried.

And as they race
the young men of Zuni
run after them.

But the Shalakos
disappear
in the distance.
They leave a strong powerful blessing
behind them, a blessing so real
it touches each person.
No wonder the Zunis feel safe.
No wonder they say:

Clasping one another tight,
holding one another fast,
we may finish our roads together.

May our roads be fulfilled.
May we grow old.
May our people's roads all be fulfilled.

41

Farther south
the Yaqui Indians have roamed
from the Yaqui River cane banks
high into the Sierra Madres
and down again through
hot dry deserts.

No matter what they have to
leave behind,
they take
their ceremonies
with them.

Their Deer Dance goes
wherever Yaquis go.

It holds the oldest
memories
of that tribe
for it was made
by hunters
to honor the deer,
to please the deer
so greatly
that he would
understand
man's need
and let himself be caught
so man could live.

The dance hasn't changed.
The flute music hasn't changed.
The rattles and the drum
and the masks
are still the same.

42

Yaqui masks are powerful—
so powerful
a Pascola dancer
turns his mask
to the side of his head
until the moment
he begins to dance.

And the Deer Dancer
wears the deer head
only when its own special music
is heard.

Like any deer
hiding in any rocky canyon
on any mountainside,
the Deer Dancer crouches,
listening for danger.
His shoulders twitch
to sounds, to smells.

He trembles.
He leaps.

The dancer feels himself
that deer.
They say
the dancer's heartbeat
is the deer's heartbeat.
Faster . . .
Faster . . .
You feel it in the music
all night long.

You wonder
if a deer
can hear
those chants:

*Little fawn, little fawn
Now coming out
From the sunrise coming out . . .*

*Plays in the rain water
Plays in the rain water.*

45

Now
think
what kind of mask
your mask
would be.

And think
what kind of songs
that mask would bring
out of you . . .

and what strange
unknown dances
your bones
would
remember

and what you would ask
and what you would promise

Now
think
what kind of mask
your mask
would be.

46

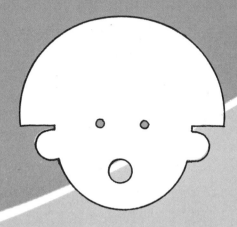

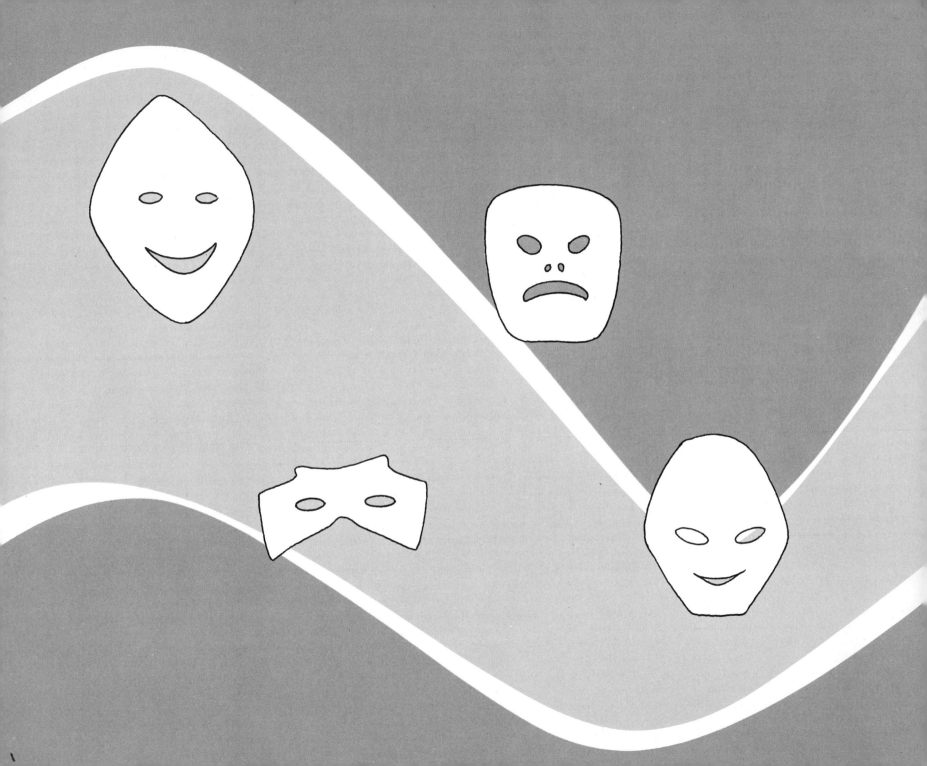

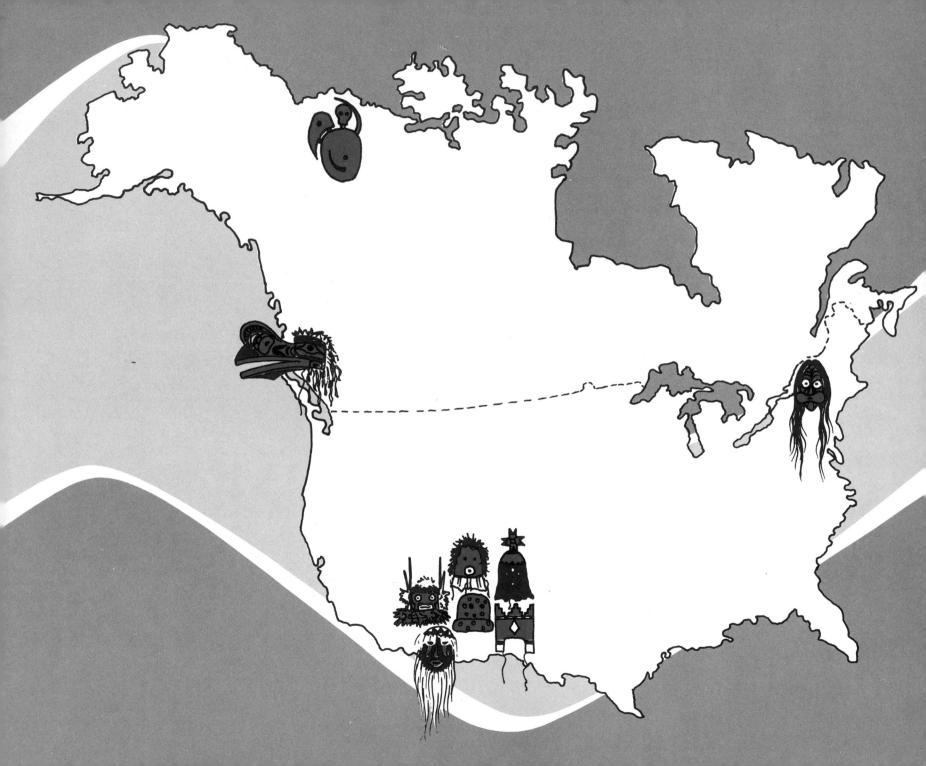